I0210953

No Fault of Water

poems by

Kelsey D. Mahaffey

Finishing Line Press
Georgetown, Kentucky

No Fault of Water

Copyright © 2026 by Kelsey D. Mahaffey
ISBN 979-8-89990-307-6 First Edition
All rights reserved under International and Pan-American Copyright Conventions.
No part of this book may be reproduced in any manner whatsoever without written
permission from the publisher, except in the case of brief quotations embodied in
critical articles and reviews.

ACKNOWLEDGMENTS

Sincerest gratitude to the editors of the following journals in which the below poems
first appeared, sometimes in slightly different versions (or with different titles):

Cumberland River Review: "Redemption"
Deep South Magazine: "Night Pawn," "Pilgrimage," and "Emergency"
Eunoia Review: "Urge to Flee on a Sunday Morning," "Have Mercy," "Rehab Rules:
Phone Calls Only," and "Wonder Valley"
Halfway Down the Stairs: "Undertow"
Minerva Rising Press: "Birthing Space"
Pinch: "The Last Monsoon"
SHIFT: "Hush," "Consumption," and "Already Gone"
Soul Forte: A Journal for Spiritual Poetry: "Mud-bound"
SWING: "Dog Days" and "The truest papaya I ever meet"
The Sunlight Press: "Solstice"

Publisher: Leah Huete de Maines
Editor: Christen Kincaid
Cover Art: Kelsey D. Mahaffey
Author Photo: Tamara Reynolds, Tamara Reynolds Photography
Cover Design: Elizabeth Maines McCleavy

Order online: www.finishinglinepress.com
also available on amazon.com

Author inquiries and mail orders:
Finishing Line Press
PO Box 1626
Georgetown, Kentucky 40324
USA

Contents

For J.
Es muss sein.

Undertow

When the flood of shadows came for you,
they came bearing gifts of night. I couldn't see
the black waters rising, gently rocking our bed.
But they knew your name, and sang to you—
soothing promises I could never make.
How weary your arms must have been,
straining to hold the light. How easy then to slip—
that warm womb sinking you like a lullaby.
Devoured by silhouettes, and in the morning,
gone.

Alcohol affects every part of the body.
Liver, stomach, eyes, brain.
Heart.
—Lisa Dordal, "Water Lessons"

You better get your coat, dear.
It looks like rain.
—Elton John, "Madman Across the Water"

Chasing Sunrise

Cold, the first splash
dots my skin like a disease.

Drunk at six a.m.,
you baptize the oars, push away
from the rain-stained dock.

We're late.

Sunk inside a plastic shell,
we fight the current
upstream, the sky impatient
to fish its sun from the horizon.

Stroke by stroke, my arms ache
for a new direction.

We land on a dry bank
already claimed by bird shit & scraps,
a graveyard for gutted bits of bone.

Waking in the distance,
a bridge gleams.

Caught between staying & leaving,
you offer a broken log,
room for two to squeeze,

then crack another beer
to toast another day. Overhead,
crows bark their disapproval.

Words sound different here.
Even they arrive too late.

Solstice

There's something about the light today.
What it does to be seen—
the way it bends and creaks,
heaving through the panes.
I watch it creep over the sill and slip
inside our bed, lifting the covers
with a brazen hiss. Snaking
up your leg as if invited,
tongue flicking your soft belly
as it rises & falls, oblivious.
My toes freeze at this intruder
burrowing deep into your chest—
as if to stay, as if it knows you,
as if it's me who doesn't belong.
And you, radiating warmth
once meant for me.
Even now as you turn from me
in sleep, face beaming,
taken by the sun.

Urge to Flee on a Sunday Morning

sometimes it hooks me
    in the back of my throat
for instance, when I'm left
    standing at the stove, spatula in hand,
        watching the black
smoke swirl as it slips
    through the vent,
        escaping
twenty years and I still can't get the burner right
    there's always this lingering,
        this smell
of butter burning, a wafting stench
    dead-fish-like, bloated & swollen,
        past the point of return
but somehow the sound of water still echoes
    even on days with no rain: dripping,
        unceasing,
some evolutionary reminder
    that a part of me remains—
        still
swimming in the deep
    a place with no more
        burning,
no more gaping mouths,
    where ovens are useless
the smoke detector pulls me back
    and for a moment I find it so odd
        to exist
where my mouth is always dry
    no matter how much I swallow

Night Pawn

I find myself again, spiraling
deep underground, teeth
grinding an old dark.

What else to do this time?

Jack wakes with magic beans &
Jill comes tumbling down.
It's too late to change the story.

Bruised, I wait for night,
the way the swollen ground waits
for sun. Patterns moon above

hauling light from long-dead stars.
Waxing, waning—
it's the cycle that always wins.

Tomorrow I'll dust the ash,
set a new day, pretend
this one's my savior.

Dog Days

parched   I wake to rumbling   summer brews
dirty sheets lie   on the floor   twisted like my thoughts
simmering in the hot air   beside me   steam breeds
behind bloodshot eyes   in the kitchen   I guzzle
coffee cold   burn a quick fix   sunlight
shafts the windows   I try not to think   my children stay
underground   pretending to be cool   building forts
with sticks & dried leaves   a door slams   it's days before
the sun sets   for breakfast   you hunt wine & crack
fresh eggs   neon yolks sun inside the pan   like a timer
your pocket dings   someone blabbing   about
sunscreen   and pick-up times   in the driveway
new toys gleam   hers & his   kayaks spoon my car
neighbors gape & grin   flapping lips   like caught fish
with no sound   I blink back the blur   stifle my need
for air   I've learned not to speak   and I think
you will burn

Hush

I craft a wreath of small skeletons,
dried twigs, and plastic creeps
that crawl in the dark places
rattling beneath our house.

Before the hunger held your heart,
the children loved the fall—
the pretend scare of shadows,
when nightmares woke only in dreams.

After their therapy session,
I'll brew cocoa with marshmallows
white as my knucklebone, then
show them how to paint the ghosts

with smiles. I cut the dead flowers
with a sharpened blade, but
the stems refuse to stay.
Cursed, I fear

I'm running out of time
to shape the mouths of pumpkins
into permanent grins. Last night,
I had to dream again:

A storm chased me.
But I was a buffalo.
Someday they'll let me show them
which way they need to run.

Consumption

Water reigns. Again,
the ground gorges on the sky's loss.

Days wasted inside while weeds rage
like motherless boys.

Even my garden gone—swallowed
by their great mouth. More and more,

greed's become our daily bread,
our need for nightly prayer.

Enough. What more
can the ground hold?

We flood our newborns until
their eyes bulge and burst rivers of tears.

We see their swollen lips
and wonder why they cannot smile.

Pilgrimage

Who knows what the river intends?
A river is lost in pursuit of the sea.
It has no time for regrets.
What else is there to say? I am not a poet—
a poet is one with something to say,
and so far, no one is listening.
I could never get as close as you.
Water fills your lungs like air.
If I tapped your palm, blood would run
the color of tears. In New Orleans,
we meander the Saint-stained
streets of the Quarter, homing toward
the Mississippi. I sit on the bank
while you jump in, giddy
as a reborn sinner. One by one,
the gutter punks follow,
diving among the debris—
their outstretched arms cleansed
by another's delusion. Undisturbed,
the river carries on, missionary
in purpose, consumed
with its sacrifice to the sea.

Already Gone

after Lisa Dordal

Past the anchor, he drifts.

Where are you going,
the children shout.
Are you coming back?

He hears them,
doesn't hear them,
their voices muffled from above.

He looks beyond them
as if they were small islands
to swim around.

He sees them,
doesn't see them—
he's washed his hands of light.

Fluid now,
he lets the water sway him.

It beckons.   He follows.

He tells them not to worry;
he'll be home soon.
An underwater echo—

their father there,
not there.

The Last Monsoon
Summer, New Orleans

I.

Soon, they'll beat it out of you,
        the waves.   Trapped inside,
            you make love to bourbon
in bed while I float
        into the long gray color of now.

Open windows give rise to rain.
            Water laps
        the floorboards   like a pack
of eager tongues.   I listen and try to speak;
        fold myself into wet sheets.

If we ever get out of here
(I think we will someday)

~

This city surrounds itself with water,
            preserves its own ghosts.
        In the flooded streets,   puddles burn
reflected flames
and this is what we call proof.

The moon buoys a blackening
            sky.   Above us,
        someone is processing something—
drowning photographs in a darkened room.

            I paddle after memories—the dry,
rough scrape
of beard on skin.

~

Thirst builds

     a gulf

between us.   I grow soft.

     High tides are permanent
     and collision is mute.

Who said evolution is linear?

I claw for feathers,
swallow gills.

~

What is it again   I'm waiting
     for?   Time cycles
on endless repeat,   incessant
     fingertips
     tapping the glass tank.

     Vision slurs.

I try to pray to fire
but I'm no longer welcome.

~

It will play out—the long, last note.
     When the glass cracks.
     When the rain stops singing.
     Someday we'll land
     naked & shivering
among the shards, sputtering
into the fresh bruise of the sky.

Get up! Don't you see?
    Here,

    even the wind has legs.

II.

            Trapped
            I float

        In the flooded
            flames

                a black

drowning   room

Thirst
                        mute

I
swallow
                                    cycles
                    tip
                the glass

        When
            When
                Someday we'll land

                the sky

Have Mercy

By the time you break free,
I'll be gone. Suitcase

snapped—decision made at last,
or in this case it seems, at least.

Pot roast is in the oven, simmering on low;
clothes tumbling in the dryer, water bill paid.

Please feed the children.
It's not your fault—the way

two lives must cross and intersect,
the way a river carves its path through rock—

no turning back now.
Think of me when the trade winds

come—they have something to say.
Today when the stranger knocked,

I let her in.

Heartbreak in the Front Yard, or
The Night my Dead Grandmother Opens my Eyes

First, my deprived sigh, a relief of sorts—a captured wind
held too long, a denied breath now set free, the night
she shows me all we've lost. Then the split: a cracked chest
leaving me gasping for air. Like walking on a frozen pond
that suddenly decides to betray you. Next the wailing—
a caterwauling of cats, the screech of cicadas responding in song.
Briefly, I think of the neighbors and how this must sound:
Shouldn't someone warn them the world is ending? I remember falling,
the twigs snapping my hair, and the fireflies frantic,
losing their poor minds. And the ground so warm, a strange
sensation of hot & cold each fighting for the win—a gut punch
of fire with bursts of melting. Flooding. Body thrashing
side to side, flopping like a caught fish unable to feel
my legs, sure I'd never walk again. And the fireflies still blaring
their cacophony of light—a jury of tiny witnesses unable to speak.

Emergency

1.

You tell me there is none.
That you are happy
and all is well.

You're just hungry.
Two eggs for breakfast
doesn't cut it anymore.

There's a store, you say,
Stop there.

I turn the car volume up.
I'm playing Counting Crows
to distract you. *Remember*
"Perfect Blue Buildings?"

You nod.

Help me stay awake, I'm falling,
the speakers sing.

You don't make it to the end.

2.

We're seen right away.

You obey the strip—
the open gown flapping
like two proud flags.

You answer the questions,
refuse the water.

Sir, can you tell me what happened?

What have you had to drink today?

        Do you want to die?

3.

Alone in the exam room,
you tell me,

More.

      Again, *More.*

            Again, *Just one more before it's too late.*

Trust me, you say.
All you need is a drink.

There's a store, you say.
We passed it on the way here.

A grocery store will do.
There's wine there—get white.

Eyes teeming with desperation.

A pink pamphlet on the wall begs,
Please take one.

*Please—just one more
and then I'll stop.*

Breath escapes me.

Soon, I say,

I'm going soon.

Birthing Space

There's comfort in the crumpling.
Surrender sinks as body takes the lead.

Like the gnaw of knowing before it's known—
awake to the want that wells inside.

It's where intimacy is created,
down here on the cold floor,

cheek pressed to marble tile,
balled up tight as a fetus.

There's weeping & wailing,
and gnashing of teeth—

a primal call to the wild,
escaping. I dive into the chasm

and let the howl take me, lungs lit
for the split. With a final push

I land on the shore beyond the fear
and emerge on the other side—

an infant of my own creation,
swaddled in my own arms,

suckling at my own breast.

Rehab Rules: Phone Calls Only

I break before you do. My polished shell
crumbles through my trembling hands.

On the line, your voice cracks, weeping
like a newborn unsure of this world.

You tell me you can't sleep without me,
of your new roommate, and the night before

clanging against the door as they drug him in
still dirty from the streets. You tell me

there are no locks on your bathroom door,
how shoelaces and belts are forbidden,

how others spill their stories
until you realize they are your own.

I want to ask about this world
without—what will hold you up?

I'd like to tell you about my walk today
in the park, how the riverbed was so dry

it smelled of rotting fish. How
I found a cardinal feather torn,

battered by god-knows-what—
filaments separated to let the light through.

I want to show you my shattered shell,
explain how I just couldn't keep it

together anymore—how
I'm desperate to hold on

to this sticky, gelatinous mess.
But what words are there for this?

Too soon, our time ends.

Mud-bound

The first step is to remove your shoes.
    Nothing is more freeing

than the introductory squish
    between the toes, the ground

remembering you with its lover's kiss.
    That magic mixed from liquid and lack—

a gift for the black-winged beauties
    to baptize their tongues.

Even the pigs understand. Nothing
    feels better than *slosh*, or *ooze*,

rolling along the lips, cooling
    pink skins with liquid brown silk.

Forget all fear of worms.
    When it's their time to crawl,

the body no longer minds.

Turning the Tide

Tonight you bring me the moon—
    her belly full & unbuckled, midnight
      scars on display. Beaming back

through the glass, this radiant glutton
    hungers for my stare. And
      when the trade winds gust,

they storm sudden & sharp,
    like French Quarter horns
      pulsing against the walls,

like your breath beating
    at the back of my neck
      as I silently gape through the lens.

What comes over us, these nights
    the moon floods our room
      and pulls us in with her tide?

Nights when she dares us
    to lap it all up—her oceans
      abandoned in the morning.

The truest papaya I ever meet

sits rank with want, roasting
at an outdoor market in the Havana sun
too far gone for the flies.

Eager to belly the blade,
her skin nearly bursts at the touch
of cold, brushed steel.

I scrape her blood-
orange walls, fleshing membranes
deep into delight, then spoon

the bruised seeds into the sink.
Lips wet for the taste,
her meat in my mouth, tongue

licked by a thousand sunsets.

Second First Date

Do you remember that night in the cafe
with the doors flung open like Cuba?
The evening air sweat our skin sweet,
the breeze unable to resist. Nearby,
a saxophone swelled and we floated on notes
an octave higher than the rest.
In your water glass, ice cubes drifted
side by side, small bodies melting into one.
Your fingers smoothed an empty cocktail napkin
like a longing re-learned; a flickering scent
of earlier and the way they held my cheek.
Candlelight hunted the shadows from your face,
and when your eyes found mine,
Listen, you said, *we know this song.*

Redemption

I could've died on that hill. My own
knife staked to the right side—heart

nailed to that cross. I hunted and gathered
the sharpest stones for the task, and polished

my favorite blade—proud of my strength.
I ranted and raged, clawed my way to the top,

only to find there was no mountain, nothing left
to stake my claim. Nothing now

to stand on but the shore of an empty lake,
the sky cloudless—a deep impossible blue.

I wade through fields of dandelions,
heads roaring in the light, and find you

on the other side, digging in the dirt.
Eyes grave like you can't leave the night.

Hauls of stones pile up from below—
an offering of jagged rock.

What use is justice now when now just is?

Here, dust your knees and take my hand,
rest beside me in the light.

We are yellow weeds rising from the ash.
We are the ash rising yellow weeds.

The stillness will come if we let it.
If we sync to its deafening,

the wind will anchor and sigh:
What use of so many stones but to build?

Wonder Valley

It's summer again when we make it
to the high desert. Legs spread,

our new homestead straddles five acres,
nothing to see but sky.

We hawk the land with eyes charred,
our dreams too small to fit—

capturing freedom
by the skin of our teeth.

We chase lizard casings from hiding
places, and feast with Captain Beefheart,

preying on sun, store-bought charcuterie,
and smoke. At night,

we toast the wind and drink the stars,
necks craned to the sky.

Surging constellations knock us back,
and rising from the cold ground

we laugh—ribcages rattling—
unsure if we'd been asleep

inside or out.

Kelsey D. Mahaffey is a certified listener poet with The Good Listening Project. Poetry pulled her from a dark corner, and she hasn't stopped writing since. Her work can be seen in: *Pinch, Deep South Magazine, SWING, Arkansas Review, Pensive: A Global Journal for Spirituality & the Arts, The Sunlight Press, Halfway Down the Stairs, Cumberland River Review, Writers Resist, Hard Candy,* and *Eunoia Review.* When she's not writing, you can find her barefoot on the back trails of her favorite park. Find more at *www.kelseydmahaffey.com.*

www.ingramcontent.com/pod-product-compliance
Lightning Source LLC
Chambersburg PA
CBHW022056080426
42734CB00009B/1377